THERE MUST BE
SOMETHING MORE!

THERE MUST BE SOMETHING MORE!

SID ROTH

ISBN 13: 978-0-7684-1059-4

Printed in the U.S.A

7 8 9 10 11 / 22

DEEP INSIDE I FELT A YEARNING—THERE HAD TO BE SOMETHING MORE!

"Because I work, eat, sleep, and that's the way it goes. There must be something more!"

These are the words of a song that I wrote shortly after graduating from college.

I BELIEVED IN GOD, BUT I FELT HE WAS A MILLION MILES AWAY AND TOO BUSY TO CARE ABOUT ME PERSONALLY. HE GRADUALLY BECAME

IRRELEVANT IN MY LIFE.

It seems as though I blinked my eyes, and I was married. I blinked my eyes again, and I had a daughter. I blinked my eyes again, and I had a job as a stockbroker with the largest brokerage firm in the world, Merrill Lynch. But there was something missing. Deep inside I felt a yearning—there had to be something more!

I couldn't find it in religion. My parents were Jewish. We attended an Orthodox synagogue where I was bar mitzvah. I was proud of being a Jew. But I found the services at the synagogue boring. I believed in God, but I felt He was a million miles away and too busy to care about me personally. He gradually became irrelevant in my life.

So I looked to money for happiness. My goal was to become a millionaire by age 30. But I blinked my eyes again, and I was 29 with no hope of being a millionaire by 30.

I left my wife, my daughter, my job, and went searching for something more. I had been married young. Perhaps the single life would give me satisfaction. After one year, I knew this was not my answer.

Then I took a New Age meditation course. The instructor taught me how to lower my brain waves. When I was in this passive, hypnotic state, I was told to invite a "counselor" into my head. He said this counselor would answer my questions.

On the last day of the course, the instructor tested my new power by giving me the name of a woman I didn't know.

I LEFT MY WIFE, MY DAUGHTER, MY JOB, AND **WENT SEARCHING FOR SOMETHING MORE.** AFTER ONE YEAR, I KNEW THIS WAS **NOT MY ANSWER.**

Then he asked me what was physically wrong with her. I asked the counselor who was in my head, and he showed me that this woman had cancer of the breast. "Could she have cancer of the breast?" I asked. My answer was correct. I knew it was not a lucky guess.

The power started growing. One day I had the thought, *I would like to open my own investment business.* Almost immediately, a businessman whom I barely knew offered me a free office, secretary, and telephone.

Soon after I took advantage of his offer, he asked, "Sid, did you know your own Jewish Bible condemns your involvement in the occult?" He showed me from the Torah, Deuteronomy 18: 10-12:

There shall not be found among thee anyone who causeth his son or his daughter to pass through the fire [child sacrifice], one who useth divination [fortune telling], one who is an observer of times [astrology], or an enchanter [sorcery or omens], or a conjurer [hypnotist, witch]. Or a charmer [casts a magic spell], or a consulter with familiar spirits [medium or someone using chan-neling or ouija boards], or a wizard [spiritist, Transcendental Meditation, Silva Mind Control, Edgar Cayce], or who inquireth of the dead [channeling, séances, etc.]. For an abomination unto the LORD are all that do these things....

This businessman told me that the "counselor" who gave me information was a demon and very evil.

THE BIBLE, THE SUPERNATURAL, AND THE JEWS

Then I read a book by McCandlish Phillips called *The Bible, the Supernatural, and the Jews.*[1] Phillips said that because a Jew is under a covenant with God, he faces an even worse judgment for participating in New Age practices. The book included stories of famous Jewish people who had dabbled in the New Age—and lost their lives.

I decided I had better find out if the Bible really was from God. So I stopped consulting the counselor in my head and started reading the Bible. I soon got the scare of my life. My counselor started

THIS BUSINESSMAN TOLD ME THAT THE "COUNSELOR" WHO GAVE ME INFORMATION WAS A DEMON AND VERY EVIL.

I SOON GOT THE

SCARE OF MY LIFE.
MY COUNSELOR STARTED

CURSING ME.

cursing me. I realized this counselor had a mind of its own and was from the pit of hell. I *had* to get rid of it. But there was no one I could go to for help.

Then things got worse. I broke into astral projection. This is when your spirit leaves your body. I was afraid my spirit would be unable to find its way back and that my body would be buried alive.

As a young boy I had a great fear of death because I thought that dying meant I would cease to exist. Now death looked like my only way to find relief from this horrible situation.

THE WORST NIGHT OF MY LIFE

The businessman who gave me the free office was a believer in Jesus. He told me that Jesus was my Messiah and would help me in my time of

NOW DEATH LOOKED LIKE MY ONLY WAY TO FIND RELIEF FROM THIS **HORRIBLE SITUATION.**

crisis. He handed me a booklet that explained my need for a Messiah. It said all men lost their ability to have experiential knowledge of God when Adam sinned in the Garden of Eden. Adam knew God as his Father and could hear God's voice. Adam walked and had intimate friendship with God. This is what all humans forfeited when Adam sinned. Their new DNA came from Adam and was a sin nature.

God chose for the Messiah to come to earth as a human (a Jewish man) to restore our God DNA, to restore us to what Adam had before his fall. Before the Messiah came, we Jewish people could have our sins covered at Yom Kippur (Day of Atonement) through an animal sacrifice in the Temple by a High Priest entering the Holy of Holies once a year. Since Ezekiel 18:4 says, *"the soul who sins shall die,"* the lamb died in our place. But the lamb was only a shadow of the Messiah. Every year we needed this sacrifice or our sins would not be forgiven.

Today, since there is no Temple or High Priest or animal sacrifice in the Temple, we are stuck with our sins. That's why we need a Messiah. The Jewish prophet Daniel wrote in Daniel 9:26 (NKJV):

> *Messiah [the Anointed One] shall be cut off [die], but not for Himself [He was sinless but shed His blood for our sins]; and the people of the prince who is to come shall destroy the city [Jerusalem] and the sanctuary [Temple].*

The Temple was destroyed in A.D. 70.

EVERY YEAR WE NEEDED THIS SACRIFICE OR OUR **SINS WOULD NOT BE FORGIVEN.**

THE TORAH
CLEARLY SAYS YOU
CANNOT HAVE

YOM KIPPUR
WITHOUT AN ANIMAL
SACRIFICE IN THE
TEMPLE BY

A HIGH PRIEST.

The booklet continued, "According to prophecy, the Messiah had to come before the Temple was destroyed in A.D. 70 and shed His blood only once. Our High Priest is now in heaven. This is why we do not need a High Priest or manmade Temple on earth. By belief in Messiah's death and resurrection," the booklet said, "our sins could be atoned for and we would get a new DNA." Our ability to have experiential knowledge of God would be restored.

The Torah clearly says you cannot have Yom Kippur without an animal sacrifice in the Temple by a High Priest. Leviticus 17:11 says:

> For the life of the flesh is in the blood, and
> I have given it to you on the altar [in the
> Temple] to make atonement for your

lives; for it is the blood that makes atone-

ment for the soul.

The choice in A.D. 70 is the same choice we have today. Either believe the Messiah was our final Yom Kippur sacrifice or believe in a different version of Judaism. One group of Jews followed Jesus 2,000 years ago and another reinvented Judaism. One group followed Messiah and the other followed Rabbinic Judaism. Later, so many Gentiles followed the Jewish Messiah that believing in Jesus came to be thought of as a Gentile religion. Originally the Messiah came only to the Jew, but His plan was to use the Jews to redeem the world!

Then the booklet said if I would tell the Messiah I was sorry for my sins and believe the blood

ORIGINALLY THE **MESSIAH CAME ONLY TO THE JEW**, BUT HIS PLAN WAS TO USE THE JEWS TO **REDEEM THE WORLD!**

SEVERAL NIGHTS LATER, ON THE WORST NIGHT OF MY LIFE, I PRAYED A TWO-WORD PRAYER: **"JESUS, HELP!"** I STILL DIDN'T KNOW IF **HE WAS REAL,** BUT I HAD NOWHERE ELSE TO TURN. WHEN I WENT TO BED, I DIDN'T WANT TO WAKE UP. **LIFE WAS TOO HARD.**

of Messiah would not just cover but totally remove my sins, I could have this new God DNA.

I had nothing to lose and said the suggested prayer that is reprinted in the back of this book. When I said the prayer nothing happened. No flashes of lightning, not even one feeling. And I thought it did not work. But God heard me, and that prayer opened the door for God to change my DNA!

Several nights later, on the worst night of my life, I prayed a two-word prayer: "Jesus, help!" I still didn't know if He was real, but I had nowhere else to turn. When I went to bed, I didn't want to wake up. Life was too hard.

The next morning I knew immediately something was different. The evil that had been inside of me was gone. I knew it had to do with that prayer. Suddenly I realized I had no fear. Instead, I felt surrounded by liquid love. This love was so pure. Finally I had experienced what the New Age could never give me—the tangible presence of God. I had never felt such peace. And I was convinced that Jesus was my Messiah.

Next I heard the audible voice of God. He told me to return to my wife and daughter. My wife, Joy, had become an agnostic when she was exposed to atheistic professors in college. But when I showed her the predictions about the Jewish people written thousands of years in advance in the Bible, she said, "I must believe the Bible is from God." She became a believer in Jesus shortly thereafter.

NEXT I HEARD **THE AUDIBLE VOICE OF GOD.** HE TOLD ME TO **RETURN TO MY WIFE AND DAUGHTER.**

My mother, **A GREAT PEACEMAKER,** CONVINCED MY FATHER THAT MY NEWFOUND **BELIEF IN JESUS WAS A PHASE** AND IT TOO **WOULD PASS.**

SOMETHING WRONG
WITH THE RABBI

My mother, a great peacemaker, convinced my father that my newfound belief in Jesus was a phase and it too would pass. I was very concerned for my parents to know the Messiah, and I tried to share my faith at every opportunity. My mother would listen, but my father would just get angry and refuse to listen. Over the years my parents watched how my marriage was restored. They observed the new stability in my life. They could see I was becoming a real *mensch* (Yiddish word that, roughly translated, means "a good person"). They watched my wife, daughter, sister, brother-in-law, and nephews become believers in Messiah Jesus. When my sister lost her infant daughter, Cheryl Ann, my parents observed her inner strength in dealing with this tragedy—a strength she had not had previously.

One day, after much prayer, my father let me read to him the 53rd chapter of Isaiah. This is the clearest prediction (written 700 years before Jesus came to earth) describing how to recognize the Messiah in the Jewish Scriptures. (Read Isaiah 53 at end of this booklet.) By the time I finished, he was angry and accused me of reading from a Christian Bible because he said I was reading about Jesus. I told him the Bible I was reading from was the same as the Jewish Bible but it included the New Testament. For him that was not good enough. He said he would only accept a Bible from his Orthodox rabbi. *Hmm,* I thought, *My father thinks Isaiah is speaking of Jesus.*

HE WAS ANGRY AND ACCUSED ME OF READING FROM A CHRISTIAN BIBLE BECAUSE HE SAID **I WAS READING ABOUT JESUS.** I TOLD HIM THE BIBLE I WAS READING FROM WAS THE **SAME AS THE JEWISH BIBLE.**

Now he had only two choices. Either he had to **AGREE JESUS WAS THE MESSIAH,** or he had to think something was wrong with the rabbi. To my shock, he said, "I've always thought there was **SOMETHING WRONG** with that rabbi."

So the next day I called our family rabbi for an appointment. When I entered his office, he greeted me with a warm welcome and asked what he could do for me. I asked if he would give me a Bible and inscribe something personal to me. He gladly complied, writing some kind words to me on the inside cover.

I thanked him and left quickly. I could not wait to show this powerful gift to my father. When I arrived, I confidently displayed the inscription to my dad and made sure he read it. Then I began to read the same passage from Isaiah. Now he had only two choices. Either he had to agree Jesus was the Messiah, or he had to think something was wrong with the rabbi. To my shock, he said, "I've always thought there was something wrong with that rabbi." And then he proceeded to tell me how he once saw the rabbi eating out in a restaurant on Yom Kippur—our day of solemn fasting.

THINK FOR YOURSELF

One afternoon when I went over to my parents' house for a visit, my father was at the racetrack. I decided this was the time to prove to my mother that Jesus was the Messiah. I knew that she had very little knowledge of the Scriptures, did not know if they were true, and gave no thought to an afterlife, although she came from a religious family and attended an Orthodox synagogue.

I started by trying to prove that there is a God and the Bible is His book: "Mom, did you know the

THE ENTIRE HISTORY OF THE JEWISH PEOPLE— **PAST, PRESENT, AND FUTURE**—IS IN THE BIBLE. HUNDREDS OF PRECISE PREDICTIONS HAVE COME TRUE ALREADY. AND THE SCIENTIFIC DATING OF THE DEAD SEA SCROLLS IN ISRAEL PROVES **NO ONE ENTERED THESE PREDICTIONS** IN THE BIBLE AFTER THE EVENT OCCURRED.

entire history of the Jewish people—past, present, and future—is in the Bible? Hundreds of precise predictions have come true already. And the scientific dating of the Dead Sea Scrolls in Israel proves no one entered these predictions in the Bible after the event occurred.

"For instance, God said He would bless us beyond any people that ever lived, if we would be obedient to His laws:

> *If you will diligently obey the voice of the LORD your God, being careful to do all His commandments which I am commanding you today, then the LORD your God will set you high above all the nations of the earth* (Deuteronomy 28:1).

"However, if we disobeyed, we would lose our country, be persecuted and scattered to the four corners of the earth:

> The LORD will bring you and your king, which you will set over you, to a nation which neither you nor your fathers have known, and there you will serve other gods, wood and stone. You will become a horror, a proverb, and an object of ridicule among all nations where the LORD shall lead you (Deuteronomy 28:36-37).

"And wherever we would flee, we would be persecuted:

> Among these nations you will find no ease, nor will the sole of your foot have rest. But there the LORD will give you

AGAINST IMPOSSIBLE ODDS, GOD HAS PRESERVED US AS A DISTINCT PEOPLE.

a trembling heart, failing of eyes, and despair of soul (Deuteronomy 28:65).

"Even though many of us would suffer and die, we would always be preserved as a distinct people:

> *Thus says the LORD, who gives the sun for a light by day and the ordinances of the moon and of the stars for a light by night, who stirs up the sea so that the waves roar, the LORD of Hosts is His name: If those ordinances depart from before Me, says the LORD, then the seed of Israel also will cease from being a nation before Me forever* (Jeremiah 31:35-36).

"With the suffering we have gone through as Jews, you would think every Jew left alive would have assimilated as a means of self-preservation.

But against impossible odds, God has preserved us as a distinct people.

"Then in the last days a miracle would happen. Israel would become a Jewish nation:

> *Therefore, surely the days are coming, says the LORD, that it will no longer be said, 'As the LORD lives, who brought up the sons of Israel out of the land of Egypt,' but, 'As the LORD lives, who brought up the sons of Israel from the land of the north and from all the lands wherever He had driven them.' And I will bring them again into their land that I gave to their fathers* (Jeremiah 16:14-15).

"If there were no Israel and the UN had to vote on it becoming a Jewish homeland today, what

GOD CAUSED A **GREAT SIGN TO OCCUR** THAT WAS OF **FAR GREATER** MAGNITUDE THAN THE CROSSING OF THE RED SEA AS THOUGH IT WERE DRY LAND. AND **A NATION, ISRAEL,** WAS FORMED **IN A DAY** AS ISAIAH PREDICTED.

AMOS SAID ONCE WE RETURNED WE WOULD REBUILD THE WASTE CITIES. **TEL AVIV IS AS MODERN AND COSMOPOLITAN** AS ANY CITY IN THE WORLD.

would the probability be? Zero would be too generous. That is how impossible it was in 1948. But God caused a great sign to occur that was of far greater magnitude than the crossing of the Red Sea as though it were dry land. And a nation, Israel, was formed in a day as Isaiah predicted:

> *Who has ever heard of such things?*
> *Who has ever seen things like this? Can*
> *a country be born in a day or a nation*
> *be brought forth in a moment?...* (Isaiah
> 66:8 NIV).

"Amos said once we returned we would *rebuild* the waste cities:

> *And I will bring my people Israel back*
> *from exile. They will rebuild the ruined*
> *cities and live in them. They will plant*

vineyards and drink their wine; they will

make gardens and eat their fruit (Amos

9:14 NIV).

"Tel Aviv is as modern and cosmopolitan as any

city in the world.

"Isaiah even said the desert would blossom as

the rose:

The wilderness and the solitary place

shall be glad, and the desert shall rejoice

and blossom as the rose (Isaiah 35:1).

"By the way, did you know Israel exports more

roses to Europe than any other nation?

"Ezekiel prophesied the reforestation of Israel:

But you, O mountains of Israel, you shall

shoot forth your branches and yield

HOW DID ISAIAH KNOW 2,700 YEARS AGO THAT ISRAEL WOULD DEVELOP TECHNOLOGY THAT WOULD CAUSE UNDERGROUND WATER TO BUBBLE TO THE SURFACE SUPPORTING THE GROWTH OF **VEGETATION IN THE BARREN DESERT?**

TWO HUNDRED YEARS BEFORE CYRUS WAS BORN, ISAIAH IDENTIFIES HIM BY NAME AND SAYS GOD WOULD **USE THIS GENTILE** TO BUILD THE JEWISH TEMPLE AND **RESTORE THE CITIES IN ISRAEL.**

your fruit for My people Israel. For they

shall come soon (Ezekiel 36:8).

"And Isaiah 35:7 (NIV) tells us:

The burning sand will become a pool, the

thirsty ground bubbling springs.

"How did Isaiah know 2,700 years ago that Israel would develop technology that would cause underground water to bubble to the surface supporting the growth of vegetation in the barren desert? Since this water originates from deep within the earth, it comes out warm, allowing growth in any weather![2]

"The only way Isaiah or any of the other prophets could have known these things is if God told them. Two hundred years before Cyrus was born, Isaiah identifies him by name and says God would use this Gentile to build the Jewish Temple and restore the cities in Israel:

> *Who says of Cyrus, 'He is My shepherd, and shall perform all My desire'; and he declares to Jerusalem, 'You shall be built,' and to the temple, 'Your foundation shall be laid' (Isaiah 44:28). Thus says the LORD to Cyrus, His anointed... (Isaiah 45:1).*

"How did Isaiah know his name? And better still, how did God get a heathen to want to restore Jerusalem?

"Jeremiah prophesied that Israel would go into captivity in Babylon for exactly 70 years:

> *For thus says the LORD: When seventy years have been completed for Babylon, I will visit you and perform My good*

JEREMIAH PROPHESIED THAT ISRAEL WOULD GO INTO CAPTIVITY IN BABYLON FOR **EXACTLY 70 YEARS.** GUESS HOW MANY YEARS WE WERE **CAPTIVE IN BABYLON?**

word toward you, in causing you to

return to this place (Jeremiah 29:10).

"Guess how many years we were captive in Babylon?

"I could go on and on about the amazing predictions of the Bible that were written thousands of years before the fact, but would you like to know about our future? Since God has demonstrated 100 percent accuracy so far, it is reasonable to expect Him to know our future."

As I quickly moved from Scripture to Scripture, I could tell my mother was impressed with my knowledge of the Bible. For the first time in her life, she was confronted with the accuracy of God's Word.

TODAY, THE PROBLEMS OF JERUSALEM AND THE TINY NATION OF ISRAEL ARE IN THE NEWS CONTINUOUSLY. AND **ISRAEL WILL BE INVADED BY MANY NATIONS.** THE INVADING POWERS ARE MENTIONED BY NAME. IT WILL BE A REAL BLOOD BATH; TWO-THIRDS OF OUR **PEOPLE WILL PERISH.**

"Mom, Zechariah says that in the last days the whole world will not know what to do with Jerusalem:

> And it will be on that day that I will set Jerusalem as a weighty stone to all the peoples. All who carry it will surely gash themselves, and all the nations of the land will be gathered against it (Zechariah 12:3).

"Today, the problems of Jerusalem and the tiny nation of Israel are in the news continuously. And Israel will be invaded by many nations. The invading powers are mentioned by name (see Ezekiel 38:3-9). It will be a real blood bath; two-thirds of our people will perish:

> And it will happen in all the land, says the Lord, that two-thirds will be cut off and

die, and one-third will be left in the land

(Zechariah 13:8).

"And when there is no hope left, the Messiah will fight for Israel. Let me read it to you from Zechariah:

Then the Lord will go out and fight against those nations, as He fights in the

WHEN THERE IS NO HOPE LEFT, THE MESSIAH WILL FIGHT FOR ISRAEL.

WE WILL REALIZE, FOR THE FIRST TIME, THAT JESUS IS OUR MESSIAH, AND WE MISSED HIM.

day of battle.... 'They [the Jewish people] will look on Me, the one they have pierced, and they will mourn for Him as one mourns for an only child, and grieve bitterly for Him as one grieves for a firstborn son. On that day the weeping in Jerusalem will be...great...' (Zechariah 14:3; 12:10-11 NIV).

"Mom, do you know why we will be weeping?" I think this was the first time I paused for air and gave her a chance to speak.

"I guess because we will be so grateful for being spared," she said.

"That is partially right. But the main reason is that we will realize, for the first time, that Jesus is our Messiah, and we missed Him."

"But if Jesus is the Messiah, why don't all the rabbis believe? Sidney, I love you, but you still don't know as much as the rabbis who have studied all their life."

"Mom, the Talmud tells us that years ago, when the rabbis pondered how to recognize the Messiah, they concluded that there would be two Messiahs. One would suffer for the people and be like Joseph. He would be rejected by His own people. He is described in Isaiah 53:

> He was despised and rejected of men, a man of sorrows and acquainted with grief. And we hid, as it were, our faces from him; He was despised, and we did not esteem Him (Isaiah 53:3).

He would **DIE BY CRUCIFIXION.** David describes this hundreds of years before the **FIRST RECORDED CRUCIFIXION.**

HIS BONES WOULD **NOT** **BE BROKEN** BECAUSE THIS IS THE REQUIREMENT FOR **ACCEPTABLE** **SACRIFICES.**

"And, according to Daniel 9:26, He would die before the second Temple was destroyed (the second Temple was destroyed in A.D. 70):

> ...*Messiah shall be cut off and shall have nothing. And the troops of the prince who shall come shall destroy the city and the sanctuary.*

"He would die by crucifixion. David describes this hundreds of years before the first recorded crucifixion. David even saw the guards gambling for his clothes. And he noted that His bones would not be broken because this is the requirement for acceptable sacrifices.

> *I am poured out like water, and all My bones are out of joint; My heart is like wax; it has melted within Me. My*

strength is dried up like a potsherd, and My tongue clings to My jaws; You have brought Me to the dust of death.... They pierced My hands and My feet; I can count all My bones. They look and stare at Me. They divide My garments among them, and for My clothing they cast lots (Psalm 22:14-18 NKJV).

"David's exact words came to pass one thousand years later when Jesus was crucified:

When they crucified Him, they divided His garments by casting lots (Matthew 27:35).

"He did not die for His own sins but for *our sins:*

DAVID'S EXACT WORDS **CAME TO PASS** ONE THOUSAND YEARS LATER WHEN **JESUS WAS CRUCIFIED.**

MESSIAH'S ANCESTRY WOULD BE FROM THE LINE OF DAVID.

...we considered Him stricken by God, stricken by Him, and afflicted. But He was pierced for our transgressions, He was crushed for our iniquities; the punishment that brought us peace was on Him, and by His wounds we are healed (Isaiah 53:4-5 NIV).

"Incidentally, the prophets go on to say the Messiah's ancestry would be from the line of David:

When your [David's] days are over and you rest with your ancestors, I will raise up your offspring to succeed you, your own flesh and blood, and I will establish his kingdom. He is the one who will build a house for my Name, and I will establish the throne of his kingdom forever

(2 Sam. 7:12-13 NIV).

"The Gentiles would follow Him:

In that day there shall be a Root of Jesse

[father of David], who shall stand as a

WHY
DON'T THE
RABBIS
SEE THIS?

banner to the peoples. For him shall the nations seek. And his rest shall be glorious (Isaiah 11:10).

"And He would be born in Bethlehem of Judah:

But you, Bethlehem Ephrathah, although you are small among the tribes of Judah, from you will come forth for Me one who will be ruler over Israel. His origins are from of old, from ancient days (Micah 5:2).

"Did you know His mother was living in the wrong place until shortly before His birth? Mary had to go to Bethlehem for a special census for tax purposes at the precise moment of his birth!"

"OK already, so why don't the rabbis see this?" she asked.

"Well, they saw the predictions of the suffering servant Messiah and called Him 'Messiah ben (son of) Joseph.' But then they found just as many predictions about the Messiah reigning as King and ushering in an age of peace. They called Him 'Messiah ben David,' like King David. How did they reconcile these supposedly contradictory roles? Their theory was that there were two distinct Messiahs. But today it is clear that it is one Messiah with two appearances. First, he came to initiate the New Covenant prophesied by Jeremiah, to change us from the inside out:

> *The days are coming, says the LORD, when I will make a new covenant with the house of Israel.... and I will remember their sin no more* (Jeremiah 31:31,34).

THEIR THEORY WAS THAT THERE WERE **TWO DISTINCT MESSIAHS.** BUT TODAY IT IS CLEAR THAT IT IS **ONE MESSIAH WITH TWO APPEARANCES.** FIRST, HE CAME TO INITIATE THE NEW COVENANT PROPHESIED BY JEREMIAH, TO **CHANGE US** FROM THE INSIDE OUT.

"Since we humans are so unclean compared to the holiness of God, we always needed a mediator and the blood of an innocent animal to atone for our sins. During Temple days our intermediary was a high priest. Today our intermediary cleanses us from all sins, the Lamb of God—Jesus—who takes

THE FIRST TIME JOSEPH IDENTIFIED HIMSELF AS OUR DELIVERER, HIS OWN BROTHERS WANTED TO KILL HIM.

away the sins of the whole world. Then, when we are clean, He actually changes our DNA and lives inside of us. God says in Jeremiah 31:33:

> I will put My law **within** them and write it
> in their hearts.

"Speaking of two appearances of the Messiah, did you know the first time Moses identified himself as our deliverer we rejected him?

> The man said [to Moses], 'Who made you
> ruler and judge over us? Are you think-
> ing of killing me as you killed the Egyp-
> tian?' Then Moses was afraid... (Exodus
> 2:14 NIV).

"And the first time Joseph identified himself as our deliverer, his own brothers wanted to kill him:

*His brothers said to him, 'Do you intend
to reign over us? Will you actually rule
us?' And they hated him all the more
because of his dream and what he had
said.... 'Here comes that dreamer!' they
said to each other. 'Come now, let's kill
him and throw him into one of these
cisterns and say that a ferocious animal
devoured him. Then we'll see what comes
of his dreams.* (Genesis 37:8, 19-20 NIV).

"Jesus fits this same pattern. His second appearance will be when He comes to rule the world and
to usher in an age of peace:

*They shall not hurt or destroy in all My
holy mountain, for the earth shall be*

JESUS FITS THIS SAME PATTERN. HIS SECOND APPEARANCE WILL BE WHEN **HE COMES TO RULE THE WORLD** AND TO USHER IN **AN AGE OF PEACE.**

full of the knowledge of the LORD, as the

waters cover the sea (Isaiah 11:9).

"Today the rabbis teach us about a coming Messiah ben David, but never mention Messiah ben Joseph. I found out why when I participated in

WHAT **HE WAS REALLY SAYING** WAS HE COULD **NOT THINK FOR HIMSELF.**

a debate with a rabbi at the University of Maryland. After the debate, I engaged a young Orthodox rabbinical student in dialogue.

I asked him to tell me who Isaiah was speaking of in the 53rd chapter. He amazed me with his answer. He said, 'I can't tell you.'

"'Why?' I quickly asked. 'You know Hebrew better than I. Read it from your Tanakh (Old Covenant).'"

"'No,' he responded, 'it would be a sin.'"

"'Why?' I asked again."

"'Because I am not holy enough,' he said. 'We can only tell you what the rabbis who lived closer to the days of Moses tell us the verse means.'"

"How sad, Mom. What he was really saying was *he could not think for himself.*"

Although I thought my presentation to my mother was overwhelming, she let me know she was grateful for the change believing in Jesus had caused in my life, but was not ready to accept the truth. "What would your father say? Are you hungry? Can I get you something to eat?"

Over the years, whenever my mother was sick, I would pray for her, and God would heal her. As a Jewish nonbeliever, my mom was so proud of me she would tell all her Jewish friends that if they were sick her son would pray in Jesus' Name, and God would heal them. Before she died, she too accepted Jesus as her Messiah.

HEAVEN MUST BE A WONDERFUL PLACE

Years later, I got a call that my father was dying in the hospital. My sister, also a believer, and I went

SHE LET ME KNOW **SHE WAS GRATEFUL** FOR THE **CHANGE BELIEVING IN JESUS** HAD CAUSED IN MY LIFE, BUT WAS **NOT READY** TO ACCEPT THE TRUTH.

My father had **LOST HIS VOICE.** His body was destroyed by cancer. But a great miracle happened. When I asked him if he wanted to make **JESUS HIS MESSIAH AND LORD,** my sister and **I HEARD HIM SAY, "YES!"**

to his bedside. I felt a strong presence of God that had been on me constantly for several days. It was the same tangible presence as when Jesus first became real to me years earlier. I said, "Dad, do you remember how Mom always said, 'Heaven must be a wonderful place'? Don't you want to be with her and the rest of our family?"

My father had lost his voice. His body was destroyed by cancer. But a great miracle happened. When I asked him if he wanted to make Jesus his Messiah and Lord, my sister and I heard him say, "Yes!"

I am a very thankful person. Every member of my immediate Jewish family believes in Jesus. Joy and I have celebrated 53 years of marriage.

It has been more than 40 years since I was set free. Over time, the mind can play tricks. If this had been my only experience with God, I would begin to doubt. But I have studied the Bible for myself, and I am 100 percent convinced only one person in all of history could be the Jewish Messiah. Daily I experience the presence of God. And I have seen miracles happen thousands of times when I pray for the sick in the Name of Jesus.

Thank God there is something more!

I AM A **VERY THANKFUL PERSON.** EVERY MEMBER OF MY IMMEDIATE JEWISH FAMILY BELIEVES IN JESUS. JOY AND I HAVE CELEBRATED 53 YEARS OF MARRIAGE. DAILY I EXPERIENCE THE PRESENCE OF GOD. AND I HAVE SEEN **MIRACLES HAPPEN** THOUSANDS OF TIMES WHEN I PRAY FOR THE SICK **IN THE NAME OF JESUS.**

WE EACH MUST THINK FOR OURSELVES. AFTER ALL, OUR ETERNITY IS AT STAKE! MAY GOD GRANT THAT SOON ALL ISRAEL WOULD BE TRUE JEWS.

WHO IS A TRUE JEW?

The Talmud declares that if a voice from heaven should contradict the majority of rabbis, we must ignore that voice (Bava Metsia 59b).

A *true* Jew says that if the Torah contradicts the majority of the rabbis, we must follow the Torah. We each must think for ourselves. After all, our eternity is at stake!

May God grant that soon all Israel would be *true* Jews.

NOW IT'S YOUR TURN

Many believe they are basically "good" because they have a "good" heart. God says differently:

> *The heart is more deceitful than all things
> and desperately wicked...* (Jeremiah
> 17:9).

But God loved us too much to leave us in that condition. This is why He says through His Jewish prophet Ezekiel:

> *I will sprinkle clean water on you, and
> you will be clean. Your filth will be
> washed away.... And I will give you a*
> ***new heart***, *and I will put a new spirit in
> you. I will take out your stony, stubborn
> heart and give you a tender, responsive
> heart* (Ezekiel 36:25-26 NLT).

The Messiah came to earth the first time to suffer and pay the penalty for our sins so we could be clean and receive a new heart. He will come

HOW COULD WE **EVER HAVE PEACE** ON EARTH WITH **WICKED HEARTS?**

a second time to usher in an age of peace on earth. How could we ever have peace on earth with wicked hearts? We all need a supernatural heart transplant.

MY WIFE FELT NOTHING WHEN SHE FIRST PRAYED TO GOD FOR A NEW HEART, BUT AS TIME WENT BY, SHE REALIZED SHE HAD CHANGED AND GOD WAS LIVING INSIDE OF HER.

God wants to give *you* a new heart filled with His love and to place His Spirit inside you. Some, like me, will have a dramatic encounter when they receive a new heart. Others will accept this forgiveness by faith. My wife felt nothing when she first prayed to God for a new heart, but as time went by, she realized she had changed and God was living inside of her.

It is also important to read the Bible. I would start with the New Testament. This will cause you to grow rapidly in the knowledge of the Messiah.

To know God is everything. To have everything and not know God is nothing. If you do not know God before you die, you will not know Him after you die.

Now say this prayer out loud and believe it to the best of your ability:

"Dear God, I confess that I have sinned against You, and I am truly sorry for it. Messiah Jesus, please come into my heart and life and cleanse me with Your precious blood of atonement. Give me a new heart filled with Your love. In Jesus' Name, Amen."

TO KNOW GOD IS EVERYTHING. TO HAVE EVERYTHING AND NOT KNOW GOD IS NOTHING. IF YOU DO NOT KNOW GOD **BEFORE YOU DIE**, YOU WILL NOT KNOW HIM **AFTER YOU DIE.**

ENDNOTES

1. McCandlish Philips, *The Bible, the Supernatural and the Jews* (New York, NY: World Pub. Co., 1970).

2. From an interview with Dr. Dov Pasternack of the Ben Gurion University of the Negev on "Report to Zion," Messianic Vision radio broadcast #8 (April 1989).

THE GREAT JEWISH RIDDLE—
PROVERBS 30:4

Who has ascended up into heaven, or descended?

Who has gathered the wind in his fists?

Who has bound the waters in a garment?

Who has established all the ends of the earth?

What is His name [obviously God], and what is the name of His son, if you know?

ISAIAH 53 (WRITTEN 700 YEARS BEFORE JESUS WAS BORN.)

Who has believed our [the prophets']
report? And to whom has the arm of the
LORD [another name for the Messiah]
been revealed? For He grew up before
Him as a tender plant and as a root out
of a dry ground. [Talking of Messiah's
supernatural birth.] He has no form or
majesty that we should look upon Him
nor appearance that we should desire
Him. He was despised and rejected of
men, a man of sorrows and acquainted
with grief. And we hid, as it were, our
faces from Him; He was despised, and we
did not esteem Him.

Surely He has borne our grief and carried our sorrows; yet we esteemed Him stricken, smitten of God, and afflicted. But He was wounded for our transgressions, He was bruised for our iniquities; the chastisement of our peace was upon Him, and by His stripes we are healed. All of us like sheep have gone astray; each of us has turned to his own way [all have the sin nature except Messiah], but the Lord has laid on Him the iniquity of us all.

He was oppressed, and He was afflicted, yet He opened not His mouth [He did not defend Himself before Pontius Pilate]; He was brought as a lamb to the slaughter, and as a sheep before its shearers is silent [our Passover Lamb], so He opened not His mouth. By oppression and judgment He was taken away, and who shall declare His generation? For He was cut off out of the land of the living; for the transgression of My people He was struck. [He was sinless and did not die for His sins but ours. He was our Yom Kippur sacrifice.] His grave was assigned with the wicked [a thief died on each side of Him], yet with the rich in His death [He was buried in a rich man's tomb], because He had done no violence, nor was any deceit in His mouth. [This could be no other Jew, not even Moses, because Torah says all men are sinful.]

Yet it pleased the LORD to bruise Him; He has put Him to grief. If He made Himself as an offering for sin, He shall see His offspring, He shall prolong His days, and the good pleasure of the LORD shall prosper in His hand. He shall see of the anguish of His soul and be satisfied. By His knowledge My righteous servant shall justify the many, for He shall bear their iniquities. Therefore, I will divide Him a portion with the great, and He shall divide the spoil with the strong, because He poured out His soul to death, and He was numbered with the transgressors, thus He bore the sin of many and made intercession for the transgressors.

Watch inspiring episodes of Sid Roth's TV program *It's Supernatural!* at SidRoth.org.

To read more about Sid Roth's supernatural encounter with Messiah Jesus, answers to questions about Jesus and more information on how to follow the Messiah and see miracles in your own life, please visit:

ThereMustBeMore.Life